National Board Certification

Generalist: Early Childhood Exam Practice Questions

Mometrix

TEST PREPARATION

DEAR FUTURE EXAM SUCCESS STORY

First of all, **THANK YOU** for purchasing Mometrix study materials!

Second, congratulations! You are one of the few determined test-takers who are committed to doing whatever it takes to excel on your exam. **You have come to the right place.** We developed these practice tests with one goal in mind: to deliver you the best possible approximation of the questions you will see on test day.

Standardized testing is one of the biggest obstacles on your road to success, which only increases the importance of doing well in the high-pressure, high-stakes environment of test day. Your results on this test could have a significant impact on your future, and these practice tests will give you the repetitions you need to build your familiarity and confidence with the test content and format to help you achieve your full potential on test day.

Your success is our success

We would love to hear from you! If you would like to share the story of your exam success or if you have any questions or comments in regard to our products, please contact us at **800-673-8175** or **support@mometrix.com**.

Thanks again for your business and we wish you continued success!

Sincerely,
The Mometrix Test Preparation Team

TABLE OF CONTENTS

iv

Practice Test #1

1. One of the most important factors influencing the quality of learning and development among young children is:

    a. Background knowledge and experiences
    b. Adequate health and nutrition
    c. Intrinsic motivation
    d. Parental involvement in the education program

2. Which of the following composers is MOST strongly associated with the Romantic Period?

    a. Johann Sebastian Bach
    b. Maurice Ravel
    c. Aaron Copland
    d. Johannes Brahms

3. According to research into differences among culturally diverse parents in America's age expectations for EC developmental milestones, which of the following is correct?

    a. Assessment data are no more likely to be misinterpreted when educators and parents have different rather than the same cultures.
    b. Due to cultural variations in when children achieve milestones, educators need not worry about developmental assessments.
    c. What parents from one culture view as developmentally normal can indicate developmental delay to parents from another culture.
    d. Regardless of parental cultural background, not reaching a developmental milestone by a certain age is always a cause for concern.

4. At what age do children typically undergo the second of three periods of language/communication development?

    a. From 0 - 6 months
    b. From 6 - 18 months
    c. From 8 - 12 months
    d. From 18-24 months

5. A first-grade teacher is planning a lesson in which students will identify and compare the features of different earth materials, including soil, rock, pebbles, and clay. Which of the following activities would best promote students' sense of inquiry about this concept?

    a. Showing students pictures of different types of earth materials
    b. Having students conduct online research about the characteristics of different earth materials
    c. Asking open-ended questions about why earth materials take different forms
    d. Having students search for and identify different earth materials on the school campus

Refer to the following for question 6:

A younger child watches you pour juice from a short, wide container into a tall, thin container and concludes there is more juice in the taller container because s/he sees the juice rising up higher in the glass. An older child concludes there is the same amount of juice either way, pointing out, "This glass is taller than the other one, but

1

it's also thinner. Besides, I just saw you pour it from that glass to this glass, so it's the same amount no matter what the glasses look like."

6. The older child pointed out having observed the juice being poured from one container to another. If you then poured it back into the first container and the child used the same logic to conclude it was still the same quantity, which ability defined by Piaget would this demonstrate?
   a. Object permanence
   b. Conservation of number
   c. Reversibility of operations
   d. Secondary circular reaction

7. Which of the following best applies to EC aesthetic experiences with the element of color?
   a. EC teachers should demonstrate mixing paint colors before having children do this.
   b. EC teachers should not involve other modalities such as songs or stories with color.
   c. EC teachers should present color samples to children rather than artists' paintings.
   d. EC teachers should teach color names, not discrimination or classification abilities.

8. A third-grade teacher is planning a unit on the characteristics of different freshwater and saltwater bodies. Which of the following accompanying activities would best connect this topic to social studies?
   a. Leading a class discussion on how hurricanes, tsunamis, and floods impact the environment and human activities
   b. Having students complete a research project on how proximity to water bodies influenced human settlement patterns
   c. Creating a Venn diagram to compare and contrast the characteristics of saltwater and freshwater bodies
   d. Instructing students to identify rural, suburban, and urban locations on a map

9. The animation of letters and numbers in Sesame Street, or of objects in Spongebob Squarepants, appeals to children in Piaget's Preoperational stage of cognitive development because of their:
   a. Logical thinking.
   b. Magical thinking.
   c. Animistic thinking.
   d. Egocentric thinking.

10. EC teachers can use puppet shows to help preschoolers develop their social skills through an entertaining medium. What is true about puppet show content and guiding children's discussion of it?
   a. Teachers should not encourage being judgmental by asking if puppets are good / bad.
   b. It would be irrelevant to ask children which puppets they liked and which they disliked.
   c. This is a good way to demonstrate it is preferable to use words over aggressive action.
   d. Children can say what occurred but not what may occur next or alternative behaviors.

11. Which statement accurately reflects the philosophy and/or practice of the Bank Street Developmental Interaction Approach to early childhood education?

   a. The behaviors of the individual teacher are more significant than classroom design.
   b. Growing up in controlled environments enables children to develop self-discipline.
   c. Different activities have strong, discrete boundaries so transitions are unnecessary.
   d. Subjects of learning are changed at irregular intervals of time to promote flexibility.

12. Which statement is accurate regarding the best mobile technology applications available to teachers?

   a. They automate but do not customize many administrative tasks.
   b. They aid not just attendance and grades but also lessons, rubrics.
   c. They require other users all to have the same apps to share data.
   d. They are not safe for separate users who can access others' data.

13. Which of these is included among things educators can do to involve diverse families in EC education?

   a. If parents cannot attend meetings due to work, educators cannot help it.
   b. It is outside educator responsibility to provide transportation or childcare.
   c. School strategies are in educators' purviews, but not home-use strategies.
   d. Educators can recruit interested family members to help out at preschool.

14. What statement is accurate regarding normally developing oral language in children?

   a. There is a considerable range of ages within normal individual growth.
   b. There are no individual differences among developmental milestones.
   c. Individual children achieve oral language milestones at specified ages.
   d. Individual children all develop spoken language skills at the same rates.

15. The waltz is traditionally associated most with which time signature?

   a. 2/2
   b. 2/4
   c. 4/4
   d. 3/4

16. Of these materials, which can teachers use to help students develop chronological thinking?

   a. Only history books can be used for this.
   b. Biographies can also serve this function.
   c. Historical literature can be used for this.
   d. These are all good chronology materials.

17. A student whose parents emigrated from Puerto Rico has learned cultural background from them, but they had little formal education. After reading a brief passage in a social studies text about Puerto Rico, the student is eager to learn more about its history. Which instructional resource would offer this information and also support reading?

   a. Educational film
   b. Dictionary entry
   c. Location photos
   d. An encyclopedia

18. A second-grade teacher is planning a unit on the basic needs of plants and animals in aquatic ecosystems. The teacher wants to incorporate a hands-on learning experience that allows students to interact with and compare different aquatic habitats, but due to their location, a field trip is not feasible. In which of the following ways could the teacher use technology to create a similar active learning experience?

    a. Have students conduct online research about different aquatic habitats.
    b. Create a slideshow presentation on the basic needs of plants and animals in aquatic ecosystems.
    c. Have students participate in a virtual field trip in which they explore various aquatic habitats.
    d. Show a documentary on the characteristics of aquatic ecosystems.

19. The Alphabetic Principle is best defined as the concept that:

    a. The letters of the alphabet are arranged in a specific sequence.
    b. The letters of the alphabet are combined to spell various words.
    c. The letters of the alphabet represent corresponding phonemes.
    d. The letters of the alphabet are used to create matching sounds.

20. A prekindergarten teacher is planning a lesson on the characteristics of living things, and wants to promote students' ability to identify patterns among the features of animals of the same species. Which of the following activities would be most effective in doing so for this age group?

    a. Having students draw and label the parts of various species of animals
    b. Conducting a presentation on the life cycles of animals
    c. Showing various photographs of animals and leading a class discussion in which students compare and contrast their characteristics
    d. Bringing in a class pet and showing students how to care for it

21. For a culturally diverse preschool class, which is the best example of an instructional strategy to benefit all the children by validating their individual cultural backgrounds?

    a. Using learning materials and activities to teach greetings in all the children's family languages
    b. Incorporating the holidays observed by all of the children's cultures into the curriculum design
    c. Supplying classroom materials about diverse countries, including those of all children's families
    d. Directing the children they must accept and play for equal amounts of time with all classmates

22. A student with autism is nonverbal but is in an inclusion classroom with a paraprofessional for support. The teacher is planning a group activity with students. What is an intervention that the teacher or paraprofessional could put in place to support this student?

    a. Pair him with another nonverbal student for group assignments
    b. Tell the student to listen to other students in his group but tell him he does not have to participate
    c. Excuse the student from all group activities
    d. Provide a device to the student to assist him with communication

23. Of the following, which is correct regarding arts education in early childhood?
   a. EC teachers should focus on assigning separate art activities so children realize art's importance.
   b. EC teachers enhance learning and comprehension by integrating art into the overall curriculum.
   c. EC teachers are told by many state standards to integrate art into units but not whole curricula.
   d. EC teachers who assign art process activities should be giving children any rules or steps in advance.

24. Regarding some benefits of technology to students, what is most correct?
   a. Notes are not completed enough to copy and paste into a composition.
   b. Students need not know spelling/grammar with spell/grammar checks.
   c. Moving text around easily helps students learn to organize their writing.
   d. Students must extensively organize and edit data as spreadsheet input.

25. A student learning to vary his writing has demonstrated skill in varying sentence length. Now he is trying to vary sentence types, but he is unsure whether he is producing complete sentences or not. Which type of resource would help him with this most?
   a. Dictionaries, online and/or in hardcopies
   b. Online and/or hardcopy grammar books
   c. Word processor program grammar check
   d. Imitating sentences by authors of classics

26. Which of these accurately reflects research results about juvenile (Type 1) diabetes as a physiological influence on child development?
   a. School performance is impacted by higher blood sugar and sleep disturbances.
   b. Having Type 1 diabetes is not found to affect the quality of children's sleeping.
   c. Diabetes causer lighter sleep in children, but this does not affect blood sugars.
   d. Research has not found correlation between Type 1 diabetes and sleep apnea.

27. Which of the following is true about young children's physical activity?
   a. Children's motor skills generally develop later than their language skills.
   b. Attempting and succeeding at physical challenges enhances self-efficacy.
   c. Physical activity develops children's physical rather than cognitive skills.
   d. Only language and arts skills can give children means of self-expression.

28. When planning physical activities for young children, which of the following must early childhood educators consider to foster positive attitudes toward exercise and movement?
   a. Differences in students' learning styles
   b. Strategies for integrating physical activity throughout the curriculum
   c. The availability and quality of necessary equipment
   d. Characteristics and abilities of students' developmental levels

29. Which of the following is true about the whole language approach to early childhood literacy instruction?

    a. The whole language approach to literacy is very similar to phonics in their analytical nature.
    b. The whole language approach to literacy is quite similar in character to alphabetic learning.
    c. The whole language approach is based on the philosophy and psychology of constructivism.
    d. The whole language approach emphasizes the similarity of each child's learning experience.

30. For children with a primarily visual learning style, which material would be most effective to give them to help them understand abstract concepts and relationships?

    a. Soft clay to sculpt
    b. Dance movements
    c. Multicolor graphics
    d. Sporting activities

31. When reading aloud to students, a second-grade teacher uses a different voice to represent each character's dialogue. This strategy is beneficial in promoting students' understanding of which literary device?

    a. Personification
    b. Point of view
    c. Juxtaposition
    d. Symbolism

32. A schema is best defined as a(n):

    a. Motor behavior
    b. Intentional action
    c. Reflexive reaction
    d. Mental construct

33. In an inclusion classroom, there are multiple English-language learners (ELLs) of differing English proficiencies. How can a teacher best support these students in the classroom?

    a. Pair each ELL with a native speaker for all assignments
    b. Provide personal dictionaries and extended time to all students
    c. Make directions on assignments simpler so that all students can understand the instructions
    d. Pull ELLs out of the classroom for more complicated assignments

34. A third-grade teacher is planning a unit on forces of motion in which students will work in pairs to investigate the speed at which marbles of varying sizes and weights roll down a ramp. Prior to introducing the unit, the teacher administered a diagnostic exam and identified a few students that will likely need additional support. Which of the following strategies should this teacher implement during the investigation portion of the unit to ensure these students can learn effectively?

    a. Provide these students with a graphic organizer to fill out during the investigation.
    b. Strategically pair these students with others that can provide scaffolding.
    c. Check frequently for understanding throughout the investigation.
    d. Have these students complete self-reflection activities at the end of each lesson during the unit.

35. Johnny loves soccer and wants to join the soccer team. Though he does not particularly like football, his parents press him to join the football team. Johnny ends up joining the football team in order to please his parents. This is an example of:

a. Conditions of worth
b. Ideal self
c. Morality principle
d. Reality principle

36. Third-grade students typically receive their spelling word lists each Monday so that they can practice them at home before the test on Friday. While their teacher is pleased that the students usually receive high grades on spelling tests, she observes that they misspell those same words when writing in journals or doing classwork. How should this teacher modify her instruction?

a. Post a list of vocabulary words when the students are writing to help them recall correct spellings.
b. Integrate spelling words into writing, reading, grammar, phonics, and other activities to help students learn the words in a variety of contexts.
c. Provide more time, such as a two-week period, between tests so that students have more time to study.
d. Review the words before certain activities to increase immediate recall of correct spellings.

37. Which of these is an important element among criteria for evaluating technological and other instructional resources in schools and districts?

a. Criteria for evaluating individual instructional technology items
b. Criteria for evaluating instructional materials less authentically
c. Criteria for evaluating the practicability of any instructional unit
d. Criteria for evaluating based on national, not district standards

38. Which of the following processes used in writing is the most complex?

a. Evaluation
b. Application
c. Comprehension
d. Knowledge recall

39. A researcher is collecting data for her study on parenting. She hypothesized that countries where mothers carry their infants on their person have children who have more secure attachments as toddlers. Which method would be the most helpful in collecting data for this study?

a. Interviewing parents in the United States about their methods of carrying babies.
b. Determining methods of carrying babies and studying the toddlers in several countries.
c. Researching popular methods of carrying infants on the internet.
d. Collecting data on the number of strollers sold in several countries.

40. Of the following, which represent learning resources rather than learning materials?

a. Learning research articles
b. Learning manipulatives
c. Learning worksheets
d. Learning games

41. Young children develop many basic science concepts through everyday activities. Of the following, which activity is most related to the development of measurement concepts?

    a. Fitting wooden pegs into holes with matching shapes in a toy
    b. Pouring sand from one container into a differently sized one
    c. Seeing how many coins they have accrued in their piggy bank
    d. Separating toys into piles of cars, trucks, animals, people, etc.

42. A veteran teacher wants to learn more about available educational technology resources to improve her instruction and create a more engaging learning experience. Which of the following professional development opportunities would be most beneficial?

    a. Keep a daily self-reflection journal.
    b. Research the benefits of using technology in the classroom.
    c. Collaborate with a mentor teacher within the school building.
    d. Participate in a professional development workshop focused on educational technology.

43. A first-grade teacher has just completed a lesson on cardinal directions. Which of the following instructional activities would be most appropriate for allowing students of this age group to practice using this skill?

    a. Using written directions to draw landmarks on a town map
    b. Placing pictures of household items in the correct location on a floor plan template
    c. Using an online satellite map to locate various physical and man-made landmarks
    d. Comparing and contrasting the features of different types of maps

44. At the beginning of the school year, a third-grade teacher has students complete a simple interest inventory and then incorporates books into the class library based upon students' responses. Which of the following best describes the benefit of implementing this strategy?

    a. Building a community of readers
    b. Creating a print-rich environment
    c. Promoting student-led learning
    d. Differentiating literacy instruction

45. Which of these correctly shows the normal developmental sequence of children's writing with regard to directional principles?

    a. No knowledge; partial knowledge; reverses the direction; correct direction; correct spacing
    b. No knowledge; reverses the direction; partial knowledge; correct spacing; correct direction
    c. No knowledge; partial knowledge; correct spacing; reverses the direction; correct direction
    d. No knowledge; reverses the direction; correct direction; correct spacing; partial knowledge

Answer Key and Explanations

1. B: The quality of health and nutrition significantly impacts nearly all aspects of learning and development among young children. These factors contribute to students' energy levels, ability to focus and sustain attention in class, working memory, and emotional regulation. Further, adequate health and nutrition are necessary for proper long-term cognitive, physical, social, and emotional development. Teaching young children about the importance of nutrition and maintaining a healthy lifestyle establishes a foundation for encouraging healthy choices throughout life. In addition, teachers must know how to recognize when students' health and nutritional needs are not being met so as to provide the appropriate support and resources.

2. D: Johannes Brahms composed music in the middle to late 19th century. Therefore, Brahms is most strongly associated with the Romantic Period in classical music, which ran from about 1815 to about 1910. Bach is most strongly associated with the Baroque Period (1600-1760), and Ravel is most closely associated with the Impressionist Period (1890-1940). Aaron Copland, often is considered "the dean of American composers" and composed music in the mid to late 20th century; he would not fit into any of the above listed periods.

3. C: Research has found significant variations among parental age expectations for various EC developmental milestones (e.g., weaning, eating, toilet-training, dressing, sleeping, etc.). Thus what is normal for one culture is abnormal for another. For example, Anglo parents usually introduce and encourage drinking from a cup to one-year-olds, so an eighteen-month-old not doing this could signal some developmental delay; but Filipino parents normally have not even introduced a cup to eighteen-month-olds, so their not using cups is developmentally normal. As in this example, some developmental milestones not reached by a certain age is *not* always a cause for concern (D). Assessment data *are* more likely to be misinterpreted when the educators' and parents' cultures differ (A) than when they share a common culture. Although age expectations for milestones vary across cultures, educators *cannot* automatically attribute everything to this variation when a child could also need a complete developmental assessment (B).

4. B: Children to three developmental periods in language and communication. The first is using crying and eye contact for expressive behaviors from birth to six months. The second period, from 6-18 months, involves intentional communication. The third period is typically from the age of 18 months on, involving the use of language as the primary method of communicating.

5. D: Scientific learning and development are best supported when young children are provided with opportunities that facilitate their natural inclination to observe and interact with the world around them. Such activities foster students' inherent sense of inquiry, as they are encouraged to use their physical senses to actively explore, investigate, and make discoveries as they build understanding of new concepts. In this situation, having students search for and identify different earth materials around the school campus would promote such inquiry by prompting students to physically interact with their immediate environment. In doing so, students would learn where these materials can be found in a natural setting, and would have the opportunity to observe, touch, and compare differences between them, thus strengthening their overall connection to learning.

6. C: When children first begin to think logically, they can perform mental operations related to concrete objects. Another feature of this development is what Piaget called reversibility, i.e., the ability to reverse an operation. For example, if a child can perform addition by adding more pennies or beads to a group while counting each new larger quantity, the child can then reverse this operation to perform subtraction, removing objects from the group while counting each new smaller quantity. Object permanence (A) refers to the understanding children typically develop during the sensorimotor stage that things they have seen still exist even when they no longer see them. Conservation of number (B) is Piaget's term for conserving numerical quantity. For example, 12 pennies are still 12 whether spread far apart or clustered closely together. The scenario described involves conservation of liquid volume, not of number. Secondary circular reactions (D) comprise a substage of Piaget's sensorimotor stage when children repeat actions purposefully.

7. A: An example of a preschool lesson to give children an aesthetic experience with color can begin by reading a children's story/singing a song about colors: involving other modalities helps integrate the element of color and the subject of visual arts into EC curriculum rather than isolating them (B). The teacher then shows children a painting or other artwork, which young children can appreciate on their own levels (C). Then the teacher presents a separate display of patches (square, round, etc.) of solid colors used in the painting/artwork, asking children to name these and other colors they know, and to name any colors in the painting not in the display. After this, the teacher should first demonstrate how to mix paints, and then give children paints in the three primary colors and have them see how many different colors they can create by mixing them differently. This exercise teaches preschoolers color names, and also sensory discrimination and classification (D).

8. B: Cross-curricular opportunities enrich instruction by demonstrating the relevance of learning in various contexts to strengthen students' understanding across content areas. When social studies is incorporated into other subject areas, students can explore its prevalence and application in daily life. In this situation, incorporating elements of social studies into a science unit on saltwater and freshwater bodies helps students understand the characteristics of different water resources, as well as how physical geography impacts human life. With exploratory activities such as a research project, students can learn how proximity to different bodies of water influenced human settlement patterns, and ultimately, other aspects of civilization, such as agriculture, diet, and commerce.

9. C: Piaget defined one characteristic of preschoolers' Preoperational thinking as animism, i.e. assigning human qualities to inanimate objects. Preoperational children do not yet think logically (A). Magical thinking (B), another characteristic Piaget defined of Preoperational children, means believing that one's thoughts or words cause external events to occur. Egocentric thinking (D), another Preoperational characteristic, means seeing things only from one's own viewpoint but not others'.

10. C: Puppet shows are not only entertaining, but are also concrete ways to engage young children in viewing and then discussing demonstrations of desirable/undesirable social behaviors. Since motor skills develop before verbal skills, many preschoolers use physical aggression to get what they want instead of expressing themselves verbally. A puppet show depicting the failures of aggressive actions and successes of verbal communication can couch instructive content in a fun format. For preschool ages, teachers should ask children which puppets were good and which were bad; this does not encourage being judgmental (A) but simply helps children define socially acceptable and unacceptable behaviors. For the same reason, it is not irrelevant to ask children which puppets they liked and disliked (B). Young children can not only summarize what happened during the show, they also can and should be encouraged to predict what could happen next, and how puppet characters could behave differently (D) to exercise and enhance their social understanding and interactions.

11. B: The Bank Street Developmental Interaction approach to early childhood education believes that children develop self-discipline and self-control through growing up in the controlled environments it provides. These controlled environments require all teachers to create well-designed classrooms; hence (A) is incorrect. Bank Street emphasizes the importance of giving children transitions between activities; hence, (C) is incorrect. This approach also stresses changing learning subjects at regular time intervals to foster children's developing a sense of direction and taking responsibility for what they do; hence (D) is incorrect.

12. B: Today's mobile applications not only automate, but also customize many administrative tasks (a) for teachers. They not only make taking attendance and recording grades much easier and faster, but also enable teachers to plan lessons and create rubrics (b) more simply and quickly. They enable other users to share and access data across different devices and applications (c) via flexible user interfaces and integrated Dropbox and other storage programs. Today, good applications commonly include protection features to guard data safety for separate users (d).

13. D: EC educators can involve diverse families in their children's educations by recruiting family members who express or show interest to help out at the preschool. If parents' work schedules prevent them from attending school meetings, proactive educators can adapt by scheduling the meetings at different times (A). Proactive educators can also provide transportation and childcare to facilitate parents' attendance to meetings and visits to the school (B). Educators can also involve diverse parents by sharing individualized strategies they can use at home with their children (B) that will support and extend the strategies used in school.

14. A: Within normal development, individual children do vary (B) as to when they reach developmental milestones in spoken language. Due this variance, normal oral language development is represented in ranges rather than specific ages (C). In addition to developing at different ages within ranges, normally developing children also vary in the rates (D) at which they develop oral language skills.

15. D: The 3/4 time signature means that there are three beats to each measure, and the quarter note equals one beat. A way to make 3/4 or waltz time easy to hear is to count, "*One* two three, *one* two three" repeatedly, stressing the first beat. 2/2 (A), or cut time, means there are two beats to each measure and the half note equals one beat. In 2/4 (B) time, there are two beats to every measure and the quarter note equals one beat. In 4/4 (C) time, there are four beats to a measure and the quarter note equals one beat. Waltz time has three counts per measure, rather than an even number (2 or 4) like the others.

16. D: Teachers can use not only history books (A); they can also assign students to read well-constructed and well-written biographies (B) of famous figures in history and works of historical literature (C), which set even fictionalized stories within real historical periods and events. Historical narratives written in "storytelling" style are also good for engaging student attention while establishing chronological sequences in history.

17. D: An educational film (a) would not support reading without accompanying text. A dictionary entry (b) gives the spellings, pronunciations, parts of speech, definitions, etymology, and examples in sentences of words, not national or historical information. Photos of locations (c) in Puerto Rico, like films, inform about the country but do not support reading without additional text. An encyclopedia (d) will provide extensive information about the history of Puerto Rico, as well as other aspects.

18. C: Conducting field trips to reinforce classroom instruction gives students hands-on opportunities to interact with and explore scientific concepts in a natural setting. This increases the relevancy of learning while fostering students' natural sense of inquiry. However, physical field trips may not always be possible, and can sometimes be limited in scope. Virtual field trips can provide similar interactive learning experiences. For this unit specifically, leading students in a virtual field trip allows them to explore and compare the characteristics of aquatic ecosystems in various locations, thus providing an active learning experience that expands their understanding of the concept.

19. C: The best definition of the Alphabetic Principle is that the letters of the alphabet are symbols to represent the various phonemes (speech sounds) we use in our language. While it is true that the alphabet has a sequence (A), this does not define the Alphabetic Principle. The sequence serves as a master mnemonic to help us remember all the letters, but we could still identify letters and associate them with phonemes without it. Similarly, choice B is true but is not the definition. Choice D is the reverse of the correct answer (sounds => letters, not letters => sounds).

20. C: Demonstrating the unifying concepts of science through developmentally appropriate activities is essential for developing young children's understanding of how scientific principles apply to the world around them. In this situation, the teacher wants to promote students' ability to identify the unifying concept of patterns related to characteristics of animals within the same species. Showing photos of various animals, and leading a class discussion in which students compare and contrast their physical characteristics, fosters their ability to recognize patterns among animals of the same species. Such an activity establishes a foundation of understanding that will allow students to identify patterns in other contexts, promoting their ability to make thoughtful predictions when engaging in scientific inquiry.

21. A: Young children develop cultural identities based on their family's cultural practices. Therefore, the preschool teacher can best address the cultural diversity of the class to benefit all students by giving them materials and activities wherein they all learn greetings in the languages of all their classmates, validating the cultural backgrounds of all children in the group. Incorporating various cultural holidays into the curriculum (B) or using multicultural classroom materials (C) alone would be insufficient for this purpose. Directing preschool-aged children to play for equal amounts of time with all classmates (D) is not feasible, as it is not a kind of behavior that can be controlled.

22. D: A device is the best method for helping this student successfully participate in group assignments. Assistive technology can help nonverbal or low-level language students become more independent in the classroom. It can help them form meaningful social interactions in the classroom with other students and can increase their confidence, which will allow them to learn more. Excusing students from group work or pairing them with other nonverbal students does not help the student develop, and may even hold them back from learning new skills.

23. B: EC teachers are advised to teach art not only in isolated lessons (A), but moreover to integrate art into the entire curriculum, which is now included in many state standards (C) for early learning and is found to improve children's understanding of many concepts and enhance their learning. Such state standards recommend integrating art projects into both individual learning units and entire curricula (C). When EC teacher assign process activities in art, they should always provide the children in advance with rules and steps (D) for proceeding, and also explain these to the children beforehand.

24. C: Word-processing software programs like Microsoft Word make it simple to move text around, a distinct benefit to students learning to organize their writing. These programs also enable students to copy notes or outlines and paste them into compositions, and then easily type into them to expand them into more complete sentences and paragraphs (a). Although these programs have spell-check and grammar-check features, students cannot rely on these in place of knowing spelling/grammar (b), as they are often wrong. Microsoft Excel and similar spreadsheet programs enable students to input data without requiring extensive advance organizing and editing (d).

25. B: Dictionaries will help a student with word meanings, spellings, pronunciations, and usage, but not with sentence structure. The grammar check functions in word processing programs (c) are typically unreliable: they frequently detect some errors but not others; try to "correct" already acceptable constructions; and, lacking artificial intelligence, also lack the informed judgment of knowledgeable humans. The greatest authors (e.g., Shakespeare) frequently break grammatical rules with the expertise to do so effectively (d). Grammar books and guides (b) supply rules for writing complete sentences.

26. A: Research studies have found that children with Type 1 diabetes spend more time in lighter sleep stages than other children (B). This light sleep causes higher blood sugar levels (C), even when parents and children conscientiously follow all diabetes management practices. Daytime sleepiness and higher blood sugars impair school performance. Additionally, researchers have recently discovered a correlation between Type 1 diabetes and sleep apnea (D), wherein the individual's breathing is frequently interrupted during sleep. Studies find about one-third of children with Type 1 diabetes also have sleep apnea, including normal-weight children.

27. B: When children respond to the challenges of developing increasing levels of control, coordination, speed, strength, agility, and flexibility, and achieve success, this improves their sense of self-efficacy, i.e., of how competent they are to perform and succeed at specific tasks. Children's motor skills generally develop *earlier,* not later than their language skills (A). For this reason, physical activity can offer young children a means of directly expressing themselves as much as arts activities, and before they have developed the language skills to do so (D). Physical activity develops both physical *and* cognitive skills (C) as it requires children to develop closer, more complex coordination of their mental and physical processes, as well as to develop decision-making, problem-solving, judgment, and other cognitive skills.

28. D: Fostering positive attitudes toward physical activity among young children is beneficial in building a foundation for making healthy choices throughout life. Exercise and movement should be encouraged in the early childhood classroom and integrated throughout the curriculum. In addition, teachers must mindfully select and implement activities that are developmentally appropriate to students' age group. This includes recognizing the characteristics and abilities relative to students' physical, cognitive, social, and emotional developmental levels. Such awareness helps teachers ensure that all students can fully participate in and enjoy physical activities, promoting positive attitudes toward them. Activities that are too complex may discourage students, whereas activities that are too simple for a given age group likely will not stimulate interest.

29. C: The whole language approach to early childhood literacy instruction has its basis in the philosophy and psychology of constructivism. Hence it is not similar to the analytical nature of teaching phonics (A) or of alphabetical learning (B). It emphasizes the uniqueness of each child's cognitive experience, not similarity (D).

30. C: Children with primarily visual learning styles focus on appearances and what they can see. They can understand and learn abstract concepts and relationships best when they are given visual stimuli like multicolor graphics, pictures, colorful objects, and other visual illustrations. Sculpting soft clay (A) would help a child who has a primarily haptic or tactile learning style, focusing on textures and movements. Dance movements (B) and sporting activities (D) are also stimuli that would help children with haptic learning styles to understand and learn abstract concepts and relationships. A primarily auditory learning style could be targeted with musical recordings, which can help a child to understand and learn abstract relationships and concepts.

31. B: As young children develop reading comprehension skills, they can begin recognizing increasingly complex literary elements to construct greater meaning. Acknowledging different points of view that exist within the same fictional text increases students' overall understanding of the story structure and provides them with insight into the motivations, feelings, and actions of each character. This knowledge improves students' ability to think critically about a text because they can analyze the events that occur and evaluate their own opinions, thoughts, and judgements in response to each character. Using a distinct voice to represent the dialogue of each character is an effective strategy for introducing the notion that multiple perspectives may appear within the same story. Doing so helps students distinguish the individual personalities of each character, thus building their understanding of different points of view.

32. D: Piaget coined the term schema to define a mental construct we form to categorize various classes/groups of things we encounter in the environment. Motor behaviors (A) are defined by Piaget as part of the first, Sensorimotor stage of cognitive development, when infants respond to sensory stimuli with motor reactions. Babies begin to demonstrate intentional actions (B), i.e. purposeful behaviors, during the Sensorimotor substage called Coordination of Secondary Circular Reactions, when they realize the cause-and-effect relationships between their own actions and environmental responses. Reflexive reactions (C) or reflexes, like rooting, sucking, grasping, orienting to sounds, and vocalizing, are the earliest substage of the Sensorimotor stage infants undergo, from birth to 1 month old.

33. C: When teaching in a classroom with multiple ELLs, teachers should strive to make all instructions on assignments as simple as possible. Using instructions with simple, understandable language should help ELLs become aware of what is actually required on an assignment. These directions should be free of slang, abbreviations, and colloquialisms that might be hard for students learning English to understand. Pairing ELLs with native speakers is a good strategy to use from time to time, but should not be used on all assignments, nor should pulling students out of class regularly when harder work is assigned. Dictionaries are also helpful as a resource to provide students with extra assistance, but the teacher should first make sure their instructions are easy to understand for all students.

34. B: Scaffolding science instruction helps to ensure that students of varying needs, skill levels, and abilities receive the support necessary to succeed in all stages of the learning process. Scaffolds can be implemented in a number of ways to accommodate a variety of learning situations. Many science activities incorporate hands-on, collaborative investigations, so strategic pairing scaffolds learning to facilitate all students' participation in the process. This strategy allows students who may need extra help to build upon the knowledge, skills, and understanding of their partners to promote their own learning and development in science.

35. A: Basically, conditions of worth are an imposition by parents and others put on children to do what the parents or others want in order to be valued. This causes the child to give up her true self in order to please the person imposing these conditions of worth.

36. B: Spelling is often taught in a systematic way. Students receive words and memorize them for quizzes and tests. However, spelling is related to many aspects of language and must be treated as a dynamic subject. Integrating the words into other parts of language instruction will help students not only learn how to spell correctly, but also to recall meanings of words and various rules of English spelling and grammar. By using the same words in different subjects, the students will retain the information more readily than if they study the words intensely for one week in only one context.

37. C: According to experienced teachers, to evaluate technological and other instructional resources, more and better criteria are needed for: evaluating not just individual technology items (a), but the overall function of technology in a given instructional unit; evaluating instructional materials more authentically, not less (b); and evaluating how practicable any unit is to implement (c) considering school and classroom realities. National standards from discipline organizations (e.g., National Council of Teachers of Mathematics, National Council of Teachers of English, etc.), teacher experience, research into subject-specific assessment, AND local school district standards (d) are among the resources educators consult for evaluation criteria.

38. A: Choice A is correct as evaluation (i.e., making critical judgments about some information) commonly incorporates the processes that the other answer choices refer to and is therefore more complex than they are. Application (B) requires taking information learned and using it in new or different circumstances. Comprehension (C) requires showing understanding of the information learned. Knowledge recall (D) involves showing proficiency in information learned.

39. B: Determining methods of carrying babies and studying the toddlers in several countries would be the best method for gathering data for this study.

40. A: Articles documenting research into various learning aspects, theories, practices, results, etc., are examples of learning resources. Concrete manipulative objects (b) to assist concept and skill learning, worksheets (c) to enable practice in new skills, and games (d) making needed skill practice more fun and motivational are all examples of learning materials.

41. B: When young children pour sand, water, rice, etc., from one container to another, differently sized (or shaped) container, they are developing basic measurement concepts. Children fitting pegs into matching holes (A) are developing basic 1:1 correspondence concepts. Seeing how many coins they have put into their piggy bank (C) helps children develop basic counting concepts. Separating toys into piles according to type (D), color, shape, size, or any other characteristic helps children develop basic classification/categorization concepts.

42. D: Regularly seeking professional development opportunities is integral to continuously improving one's pedagogical knowledge and skills to enhance the learning experience for all students. Doing so helps teachers stay current in the field by exposing them to new pedagogical theories and practices, instructional strategies, resources, and learning materials. In this situation, a workshop would be most beneficial in helping this teacher become knowledgeable on available and relevant technology resources while providing hands-on opportunities to learn how to apply them in the classroom.

43. A: Providing young children with hands-on experiences to practice skills related to social studies strengthens their internalization of foundational concepts necessary for continued success in learning. Doing so helps establish a framework for reference that students can apply when learning increasingly complex topics in the content area. The ability to use cardinal directions, for example, is necessary for describing the locations of places and regions, as well as understanding more complex ideas related to geographic literacy, such as spatial awareness, latitude, longitude, and time zones. In this situation, having students use written directions to physically draw landmarks on a town map allows them to visualize cardinal directions in a hands-on, developmentally appropriate learning setting.

44. A: Fostering a community of readers in the early childhood classroom establishes a foundation for literacy skill development and encourages lifelong reading. Regularly engaging in reading builds vocabulary by exposing students to a range of new words that may not be included in the general curriculum while promoting comprehension and fluency skills. Students are more inclined to develop positive attitudes toward reading when they have access to a variety of literacy materials that align with their personal interests. To build a community of readers, it is important that teachers make an effort to learn which subjects and genres their students find most relevant and engaging. Activities such as interest inventories are beneficial in providing this information, as teachers can utilize students' responses to create a classroom library that motivates students to read.

45. A: First, a child typically shows no knowledge of the correct direction in which to write (left-right, top-bottom in English); then partial knowledge, e.g., *either* left-right *or* top-bottom *or* moving from the upper right at the end of one line to the left for the next line; then reversed writing direction; then correct directionality; then correct direction plus correct spacing between words.

Practice Test #2

1. Which statement is most accurate about the interactions of American educators with culturally diverse families?

    a. The problems are encountered primarily by culturally diverse families.
    b. The problems are encountered primarily by the American educators.
    c. The problems are encountered equally by the families and educators.
    d. The problems are encountered usually quite minimally by either group.

2. How can teachers interact with diverse students to clarify class goals and purposes for attaining communication goals?

    a. Cover all details thoroughly rather than only emphasizing major points.
    b. Avoid confusing students by comparing and contrasting main concepts.
    c. Support student comprehension by providing analogies and metaphors.
    d. Connect content topics to students' prior knowledge, interests, and values.

3. A fourth-grade teacher uses a classroom token economy in which students can redeem tickets earned for positive behavior in exchange for various prizes. The most sought-after prizes require more tickets, whereas less desired items cost less. This strategy promotes students' understanding of which of the following concepts?

    a. Supply and demand
    b. Scarcity and choice
    c. Limited resources
    d. Profits and losses

4. A history teacher has assigned his final research project of the semester. For this project, he sets the requirement of four online sources and three print sources. Over the next few days, several students express their concern over being unable to find the necessary sources to complete their project due to their lack of computer access at home. What can the teacher do to make sure all students have fair access to complete this project?

    a. Make and arrangement media center specialists for students to stay after school to gather the necessary research materials for the project
    b. Schedule time in your class period for students to go to the media center and computer lab to gather the necessary research
    c. Provide clear instructions for the project so that students know what is expected of them
    d. Pair students together so that students with access to resources work with students without access to resources

5. A third-grade teacher is planning a lesson on identifying and describing natural physical characteristics. It will include four learning stations. In the first station, students will read a passage on the topic and answer some corresponding comprehension questions. The second station will include a short video describing various landforms. Students will work together in the third station to label a map, and will draw several landforms in the fourth station. By implementing this strategy, the teacher does which of the following?

    a. Modifies instruction to accommodate students' varying abilities
    b. Provides active-learning experiences to foster student engagement
    c. Recognizes the importance of incorporating play into instruction for young children
    d. Differentiates instruction to align with students' learning styles, needs, and preferences

6. A second-grade teacher is preparing a unit on adding inflectional morphemes to words. Which phonics-related concept should this teacher review prior to beginning this unit?

    a. Digraphs
    b. Letter-sound correspondence
    c. Long and short vowel sounds
    d. Syllable segmentation

7. A fourth-grade teacher is planning a lesson in which students will read and interact with a famous speech by Franklin D. Roosevelt. Prior to beginning the unit, the teacher temporarily groups students based on reading ability. This is an example of which of the following strategies for differentiating instruction?

    a. Flexible grouping
    b. Heterogeneous grouping
    c. Student-choice grouping
    d. Random grouping

8. Which of the following is the earliest phonological feature to be independently recognizable in a typically developing child?

    a. Syllables
    b. Alliteration
    c. Rhyming
    d. Letter-sound relationships

9. A first-year teacher wants to improve how well she manages her classroom. Which approach would be most effective in improving her classroom management practices?

    a. Ask the principal of the school for the best techniques for classroom management
    b. Ask the media center specialist for books and other resources that teach effective classroom management
    c. Observe experienced teachers to get an idea of how they manage their classrooms
    d. Consult with parents about what they have found effective in managing their own children

10. Which of these is an example of attributes to seek in good children's literature?

    a. Stable story characters who do not change
    b. Books featuring overtly moralistic themes
    c. Concise summaries of race/gender types
    d. Original yet believable plot constructions

11. Which is the best definition of an informal learning experience for learning basic science concepts?

    a. A child chooses what to do, and an adult provides some intervention
    b. A child chooses what to do spontaneously without adult intervention
    c. A child engages in an activity which is chosen and directed by an adult
    d. A child engages in a group activity assigned by the preschool teacher

12. A teaching assistant identifies a "teachable moment" when two kindergarten students are arguing about whose toy is bigger. Which resource can she provide in showing them how to settle the dispute objectively?

a. Computer
b. Graph
c. Chart
d. Ruler

13. What is the best way that teachers can help make sure that proper ethical behavior related to technology is followed in their classroom?

a. Model appropriate behavior while using technology
b. Continually monitor students while they are using technology in the classroom
c. Give students a list of guidelines that they should follow
d. Give a test on proper ethical behavior to the students

14. During which age range do children's motor skills normally develop the fastest?

a. Birth to four years
b. From one to five years
c. From three to seven years
d. From two to six years

15. Which of these is true about what teachers can do using technology?

a. Teachers can communicate with parents using varied methods.
b. Teachers must hand-write their learning units and lesson plans.
c. Teachers can read and grade papers but cannot add comments.
d. Teachers cannot create rubrics as easily as they can worksheets.

16. What can preschool children learn from lessons about the visual art element of line?

a. This will not help them make better comparisons.
b. Children's symbol recognition will not be affected.
c. Children's ability to recognize shapes will develop.
d. Preschoolers cannot distinguish among line types.

17. Mrs. Eli is holding a career day for her fifth grade class of 25 students, and has invited parents to come to class and discuss their jobs. Many parents have expressed interest, but most of them have said that they will have difficulty leaving their jobs during the school day. All but which of the following technological solutions might be helpful in addressing this problem?

a. Holding the presentation by videoconference during the parent's lunch break
b. Holding the presentation by teleconference during the parent's lunch break
c. Asking the parent to create a videotape in which they discuss their job and sending it to school
d. Asking the parent to create a slide show presentation about their job for their child to present to the class

18. Prior to reading a new story aloud to the class, a kindergarten teacher leads students through a picture walk of the book. This strategy promotes students' overall comprehension by fostering their ability to do which of the following?

    a. Make connections between illustrations and text
    b. Identify the author and illustrator
    c. Use proper book handling skills
    d. Make inferences about events in the story

19. Based on the chart, which of the following statements is NOT accurate?

Jail Inmates by Sex and Race				
Year	1990	1995	2000	2005
Male	365,821	448,000	543,120	646,807
Female	37,198	51,300	70,414	93,963
Juveniles	2,301	7,800	7,613	6,759
White	169,600	203,300	260,500	331,000
Black	172,300	220,600	256,300	290,500
Hispanic	58,100	74,400	94,100	111,900

[Source: US Dept. of Justice; does not include federal or state prisons.]

    a. Fewer women than men are incarcerated in each year sampled.
    b. The rate of jail incarceration rose for every subgroup of prisoner.
    c. In 2000 and in 2005, more whites were incarcerated in jails than any other race.
    d. Rate of Hispanic jailing has steadily increased over the fifteen years represented.

20. What is the relationship between project-based learning and technology?

    a. Technology is a fundamental characteristic of project-based learning
    b. Technology should only be used in project-based learning after students are in middle school
    c. Technology should generally not be used in project-based learning
    d. Technology can strengthen project-based learning

21. A fourth-grade teacher is preparing to administer an end-of-unit test to a linguistically diverse group of students. To ensure ethical assessment practices, which of the following is the teacher responsible to provide to the English language learners in her class?

    a. The option to take the test in their preferred language
    b. The opportunity to retake the test if necessary to improve students' grades
    c. A qualified interpreter to translate the test
    d. Linguistic aids aligned with students' English language proficiency levels

22. When introducing new high-frequency vocabulary, a first-grade teacher uses a mapping activity in which students separate, graph, and tap out the individual phonemes of each new word while reading them aloud. This strategy is likely intended to promote which of the following?

    a. Automaticity
    b. Prosody
    c. Orthographic mapping
    d. Receptive language skills

23. One of the most significant factors that may influence young children's nutrition, physical health, and overall development is:

    a. Cultural background
    b. Parents' highest level of education
    c. Socioeconomic status
    d. Genetic history

24. According to Erikson, which stage of social behavior is most typical of children around 2–3 years old?

    a. Developing control over their physical skills
    b. Developing control over their environment
    c. Developing trust in parents' meeting needs
    d. Developing friendships and success at tasks

25. A first-grade teacher is preparing a lesson in which students will work in groups to investigate what happens when food coloring is added to different forms of liquids. At each group, the teacher has placed a bin with measuring spoons, cups, a funnel, and a magnifying glass. Providing these items develops students' understanding of:

    a. The connection between science and other disciplines
    b. How to follow the steps of the scientific method
    c. The purpose of scientific tools and when to use them
    d. The proper care, handling, and storage of scientific tools

26. An EC teacher has children lie down on butcher paper in whatever body positions they choose and outlines their body shapes with a marker. Then the teacher has the children enhance and personalize these outlines by drawing different kinds of lines with various tools. What is correct about this activity?

    a. The children will learn how line is used in visual art and about drawing different kinds of lines.
    b. The children will not learn as much from this activity as from shapes that are not their own.
    c. The children will learn more about how shape is used in art than about how lines are used.
    d. The children will learn kinesthetic concepts from posing their bodies but not anything about art.

27. Lead teaching, learning centers / learning stations, resource services, team teaching and consultation are all used in:

    a. Innovative teaching
    b. Strategic teaching
    c. Collaborative teaching
    d. Self-contained classrooms

28. What is most accurate regarding stereotyping in early childhood?

    a. Preschoolers naturally form stereotyped cognitions about other people.
    b. Preschoolers are not cognitively developed enough to form stereotypes.
    c. Preschoolers do not naturally stereotype others, but are taught to do so.
    d. Preschoolers do not understand stereotyping as it is an abstract concept.

29. While students are engaged in creating their own artworks, their teacher shows them other students' work. The teacher's doing this facilitates:

    a. Generalization/transfer from the creation process to the response process.
    b. Generalization/transfer from the response process to the creation process.
    c. Generalization/transfer from an analysis process to an interpreting process.
    d. Generalization/transfer from the interpretation into the evaluation process.

30. Which of the following is a valid technique to use with non-native English speakers in your class if they are having trouble and your school has very limited ESL resources?

    a. Ask the student's parents to hire a translator to sit with the child in class
    b. Use more visual aids and illustrative hand gestures while teaching
    c. Speak as rapidly as possible so that the student will get used to hearing English faster
    d. Repeat everything you say twice

31. Which of these is accurate regarding young children's development of print awareness?

    a. The most common age for children to develop print awareness is between five and seven years.
    b. Research finds that four-year-olds are likely to acquire print concepts before word concepts.
    c. Preschoolers who attain print literacy skills are no more likely to read better at later ages.
    d. Print awareness is knowing that print has meaning, but not necessarily its form/function.

32. When a toddler begins to shout, "NO!" often, Erikson would characterize this behavior as:

    a. Developing autonomy
    b. Developing initiative
    c. Developing industry
    d. Developing mistrust

33. To help young children practice the collection, organization, and display of data, which of the following activities would be most relevant?

    a. A teacher lets children choose differently shaped stickers and identify what those shapes are
    b. A teacher lets children choose differently colored stickers and guess numbers of colors picked
    c. A teacher lets children choose differently colored stickers and match them to colors on a chart
    d. A teacher lets children choose differently colored stickers as cumulative rewards toward prizes

34. When preschool teachers provide activities to develop social skills, what is true about some necessary skills that young children should and can learn?

    a. Young children learn to verbalize what they want in cooperative activities.
    b. Preschool children are too egocentric to learn to have empathy for others.
    c. Assigning collaborative projects will not teach preschoolers to cooperate.
    d. Preschool children are not yet cognitively able to learn how to take turns.

35. In a popular set of six conflict-mediation/resolution steps for young children, the first step is to approach the conflict calmly, interrupting any hurtful behaviors; the second step is to acknowledge the children's feelings. Of the subsequent four steps, while comes first?

a. Gather enough information about the conflict.
b. Elicit potential solutions; help children pick one.
c. Reiterate/state over again what the problem is.
d. Provide the children with support as is needed.

36. Children develop phonological awareness:

a. Only through direct training given by adults
b. Only naturally, through exposure to language
c. Via both natural exposure and direct training
d. Via neither incidental exposure nor instruction

37. Which of the following activities would be MOST appropriate for helping students develop an appreciation for the value and role of art in US society?

a. Having students create a slide show presentation about a famous American artist
b. Asking students to create a timeline showing when famous works of American art were created
c. Taking students on a field trip to an art museum
d. Asking students to write an essay comparing and contrasting the influence that two famous American artists or artworks had on US society

38. To be effective, what essential learning element must technology support?

a. Students must have connections with experts in real life.
b. Students must be engaged whether actively or passively.
c. Students must participate in activities via individual work.
d. Students must interact, but do not need to get feedback.

39. A second-grade teacher wants to promote students' coordination of purposeful body movements. Which of the following activities would be most developmentally appropriate in achieving this goal?

a. Having students practice throwing and catching a ball with a partner
b. Providing students with opportunities to manipulate small objects
c. Acting out finger plays
d. Having students participate in interactive group games, such as kickball or follow-the-leader

40. Students in a fourth-grade class have been assigned to read a short fictional novel over the course of several weeks. During the unit, the teacher plans to have students participate in literature circles. Which of the following best describes how this strategy is beneficial in promoting students' reading comprehension?

a. Students feel more accountable to read the book.
b. Reluctant readers can hear others read the text.
c. It provides an engaging and interactive context for reading.
d. Students' grades are dependent upon participation of all group members.

41. In the literacy corner of a prekindergarten classroom, a teacher has added pictures of familiar traffic signs, logos, and food labels. This strategy is likely intended to promote students' development of which of the following skills?

    a. Decoding and encoding
    b. Letter and number recognition
    c. Letter-sound correspondence
    d. Automaticity

42. A second-grade teacher is planning an economics lesson, and wants to develop students' understanding of opportunity cost. Which of the following instructional activities would likely best achieve this goal?

    a. A collaborative think-aloud activity in which students are given pretend money and discuss whether to save it or spend it on a desired item
    b. A project in which students create a budget and plan an imaginary trip
    c. A class discussion regarding the differences between wants and needs in a community
    d. A brainstorming activity in which students devise creative ways to earn extra money

43. Of the following, which statement is true about instruction in the alphabetic principle?

    a. Letter-sound relationships with the highest utility should be the earliest ones introduced.
    b. The instruction of letter-sound correspondences should always be done in word context.
    c. Letter-sound relationship practice times should only be assigned apart from other lessons.
    d. Letter-sound relationship practice should focus on new relationships, not go over old ones.

44. A prekindergarten teacher is leading an activity in which students use discarded items, such as tissue boxes, paper towel rolls, and egg cartons, to create art projects. This teacher is establishing a foundation for understanding which of the following environmental concepts?

    a. Recycling as a form of waste management
    b. The difference between renewable and nonrenewable resources
    c. Ways in which litter contributes to pollution
    d. How to distinguish between recyclable and nonrecyclable items

45. During Piaget's second stage of cognitive development, adults should realize that children's thinking is primarily:

    a. Logical
    b. Intuitive
    c. Sensory
    d. Motoric

Answer Key and Explanations

1. C: Both culturally diverse families and American educators experience equal problems in their interactions. Educators and diverse families both have difficulties dealing with foreign languages, different customs and behaviors, and major differences in the educational systems with which they are familiar—including different laws for special education. Thus neither the families (A) nor the educators (B) experience greater difficulty than the other. Moreover, the challenges both groups experience are not necessarily or even usually very minimal (D) in nature; they can be quite substantial.

2. C: For attaining communication goals, teachers can interact with diverse students for clarifying class goals and purposes by concentrating on major points and letting students find additional details through other activities (a); they can also achieve these goals by comparing and contrasting concepts, which clarifies them rather than confuses students (b). Connecting content topics to students' prior knowledge, interests, and values (d) as well as to student experience and the topics' utility for students is a way teachers can interact with students to stimulate their curiosity and interest rather than to clarify class goals and purposes.

3. A: Understanding the concept of supply and demand—the notion that the availability of and desire for a product influences its price—is important for developing economic literacy. This skill is necessary for grasping increasingly complex topics, such as economic interdependence, price determination, and market competition. Students learn this foundational concept most effectively when provided with opportunities to interact with it in a relevant and meaningful way. By requiring more tickets for sought-after prizes, this teacher incorporates supply and demand into the classroom token economy in a real-world, applicable context to promote student understanding.

4. B: When teachers assign projects that require the use of technology and independent research, they should ensure that all students have reasonable access to the materials they need to complete the project. In this case, if the teacher can schedule time for students to go to the media center and computer lab during class, this would help students gather the materials they need and ensure that all students have a fair chance to complete the project. Asking students to stay after school may be difficult for students who rely on the school bus for transportation or who have other responsibilities after school. Clear instructions should always be given on assignments, but clear instructions will not help students who do not have the means to complete the assignment. Pairing students together for the assignment is likely not what the teacher wants to do for a final research project that he was anticipating students complete alone. It would be best for him to make sure all students have access to the resources they need.

5. D: All students learn and process new information differently, so it is important to incorporate multiple and varied opportunities for them to do so. Differentiating instruction allows teachers to appeal to variances in learning styles, individual needs, and preferences to create an accessible, engaging experience for all students. Learning stations are an effective strategy for achieving this, as they incorporate several activities focused on different strengths, interests, and abilities. In this lesson, the teacher includes both intrapersonal and interpersonal learning opportunities, as well as activities that appeal to auditory and kinesthetic learners, to provide differentiation.

6. D: In the English language, inflectional morphemes refer to suffixes that change the grammatical tense, quantity, or possession of a word without altering the meaning of the root word itself. These linguistic units are bound to the root word and carry no semantic meaning on their own. Examples

25

include "-ed," "-ing," "-s," and "-est." As this grammatical concept can prove especially difficult for young children to master, it is important that they have first acquired strong foundational knowledge related to a number of phonics-related skills. One such skill includes syllable segmentation, or the ability to distinguish the individual phonemes within words. Reviewing this concept prior to introducing inflectional morphemes would be beneficial in reinforcing students' knowledge of word structure and emphasizing the patterns of suffixes, thus promoting their ability to decode increasingly complex multisyllabic words.

7. A: Differentiating instruction is necessary to provide students of varying needs, abilities, skills, and preferences with equitable and engaging opportunities to participate in learning. Differentiated instruction takes several forms, and should occur throughout all stages of instruction. In this situation, the teacher plans to differentiate a lesson on a speech made by Franklin D. Roosevelt by implementing flexible grouping based on students' reading ability. Flexible grouping is the temporary grouping of students to accommodate specific learning needs in a given area. This strategy will allow the teacher to incorporate the appropriate scaffolds, such as chunking or modifying the text, to ensure all students have the supports necessary to learn effectively.

8. C: Phonological awareness skills are developed over the course of several years, and where there may be overlap in development, recognition of rhymes (C) comes rather early, between 2 and 3 years of age. Recognition of alliteration comes shortly thereafter, whereas syllables are recognizable between 3 and 6 years old. Phonic understanding is much more complex, as it requires a coordination between auditory and visual understanding.

9. C: Observing more experienced teachers can be an extremely useful tool for first-year teachers to improve both their classroom management and their instructional strategies. This allows teachers to see new strategies in action and has the potential of being able to teach much more to a newer teacher than most other methods. Asking the principal for suggestions may result in a few useful suggestions, but it is likely not the most effective method for gathering ideas or strategies. Asking the specialist for books can be an additional tool to utilize for classroom management strategies, but it would not be as effective as observing experienced teachers. Consulting with parents is not an ideal way to develop classroom management strategies because most parents have not been in the classroom as educators and do not know effective strategies for managing large groups of children while teaching them.

10. D: Good children's books should feature plots that are well-constructed, and are original but not incredible. Narrative books should feature story characters who are believable, which includes their changing (A) and growing as a result of their experiences like real people do, rather than staying the same throughout the story. Adults choosing children's literature should seek books with themes of value to children, but avoid books with overtly moralistic themes (B). Likewise they should avoid books that promote racial, gender, and other stereotypes (C).

11. A: When young children learn basic science concepts, an informal learning experience is defined as one wherein the child has choice and control over the activity, but at some point during the activity an adult provides some kind of intervention. When the child has complete choice and control of the activity and no adult intervenes at all (B), this is the definition of a naturalistic learning experience. If the child's activity is chosen and directed by an adult (C), or assigned to a group of children in preschool by the teacher (D), these are examples of structured learning experiences.

12. D: Young children tend to focus on only one attribute of objects to the exclusion of others—e.g., height but not width, number of pieces rather than overall size or amount, etc. A computer (a) is overkill; a graph (b) or chart (c) is irrelevant. By providing a ruler (d) and then showing them how to measure both toys, the assistant can teach the children how to use an objective measurement.

13. B: To ensure that students are using technology appropriately and ethically in a classroom, teachers should continually monitor what students are doing when they have access to technology. This is the best way to ensure that proper ethical behavior is followed in a classroom. Modeling appropriate behavior can help reinforce how to use technology properly, as can lists of guidelines that are provided for students about how to behave. However, continually monitoring students is the best way to make sure that students act appropriately.

14. D: Children's motor skills normally develop the fastest between the ages of two and six years. From birth to four years (A), infants lift their heads and control their eye muscles; then learn to roll over and grasp; then sit up and crawl; stand and creep by one year; learn to walk, then run, kick, jump; and by three to four years can jump up and down and stand on one leg. By five years (B), they typically can skip, broad-jump, and dress themselves. By six to seven years (C), they are skillful with throwing, catching, dodging, and directing balls, and can tie their shoelaces and color pictures.

15. A: Technology enables teachers to communicate with parents in a variety of ways, e.g., via email, text messaging, Facebook messages/posts, Twitter tweets, posts on class/school websites, videoconferencing, etc. Teachers save much time and effort using word-processing software programs to create learning units and lesson plans (b). They can read and grade papers and also add comments (c): for example, MS Word has a Comments area in the right margin; Adobe Acrobat PDFs allow adding comments as electronic sticky notes. Teachers can create rubrics as easily as worksheets (d), checklists, handouts, etc.

16. C: Preschool children's ability to recognize shapes will develop through well-designed lessons focusing on line as an element of visual art. Such lessons will also help preschoolers to improve their ability to make comparisons (A) and expand their ability to recognize symbols (B). Teachers can help children identify different types of lines like straight, wavy, spiral, pointy, zigzag, etc., separately drawn on paper, which is within the abilities of preschoolers, and then ask them to find these line types in a work of art, (D), which they will be able to do after identifying them separately. Teachers can then have children draw the different line types themselves, and experiment with different line-drawing tools.

17. B: Conducting a teleconference with the parent while they're on their lunch break would probably not be effective because it would require students to gather around one speakerphone or each have their own phones. A videoconference could be arranged so all of the students can easily see the parent and the parent can see the students and respond to their questions, and slide show or videotaping would also be effective at conveying the information if videoconferencing technology was not available.

18. A: Familiarizing young children with the illustrations in a story prior to reading the text is highly beneficial in promoting overall comprehension. Doing so helps emergent readers formulate connections between pictures and corresponding text, thus promoting their ability to make predictions, sequence events, recall major details, and grasp the meaning of unfamiliar vocabulary. Activities such as picture walks, in which students are shown and prompted to discuss the illustrations in a story prior to hearing it read aloud, are an effective method for building students' background knowledge and providing context to establish the foundation necessary for greater overall comprehension.

19. B: The rate of incarceration for juveniles did decrease after 1995. Answer A is a correct statement. Fewer women than men are incarcerated in each year sampled, even though the number of females incarcerated is growing. Response C is also accurate; in the years specified, more whites were incarcerated in jails than any other race. The chart clearly shows an increase in the number of Hispanics being jailed, making response D an accurate statement.

20. D: Technology is a tool that, when used properly, can strengthen project-based learning in the classroom. When teachers incorporate good technological tools into class, it can greatly strengthen the learning that occurs, and make students more independent. While not all project-based learning projects will use technology, a great number of them are likely to use it at least some for students to gather the necessary materials. With proper supervision and education, elementary school students should be able to use technology in project-based learning just as well as middle and high school students.

21. D: Teachers have the professional and ethical responsibility to provide all students with a fair and equitable testing environment. As such, some students may require special accommodations to facilitate their ability to demonstrate mastery of a skill or concept. For ELL students, this entails implementing linguistic supports aligned with their levels of English language proficiency. Doing so supports these students' comprehension of testing material, allowing them to successfully complete the assessment.

22. C: Orthographic mapping refers to a process that occurs when the reader uses knowledge of letter-sound correspondence to recognize and recall the spelling, pronunciation, and meaning of written words. This process is necessary to build the word recognition skills and automaticity necessary for developing reading fluency. When introducing new vocabulary, teachers can stimulate orthographic mapping by having students separate the words into individual sounds to demonstrate the phonemic-graphemic relationship. This strategy helps students commit new words to memory, thus promoting vocabulary acquisition and sight word recognition. Further, having students tap out each phoneme as they read it aloud adds a kinesthetic element, thus strengthening connections for greater understanding.

23. C: Socioeconomic status may have significant implications on the quality of children's nutrition, physical health, and overall development. Families from low-income backgrounds often face several obstacles that may prevent access to resources and education related to adequate nutrition and health practices. This places children at greater risk for experiencing hindered development across domains, including cognitive delays, slowed physical growth, illness, and social, emotional, and behavioral issues. Further, as the foundation for nutrition, health, and fitness practices are often instilled in early childhood, those from socioeconomically disadvantaged backgrounds may be less likely to adopt healthy practices as they develop. If it is suspected that a student is in such a situation, it is important to refer the family to school- and community-based resources that can provide assistance.

24. A: In Erikson's theory of psychosocial development, infants from birth to around 18 months learn to develop trust or mistrust in parents' meeting their needs (C) fully and consistently or not. Children aged around 2–3 years, engaged in toilet training and asserting their independence, are developing control over their personal physical skills. Preschoolers aged around 3–5 years, exploring the world around them, are developing and asserting their control over the environment (B). Children beginning school around 6 years old are engaged in learning to form new friendships and other social relationships, and learning to address the demands of new tasks at school (D).

25. C: Supporting students' learning and development in science includes helping them understand the purpose of scientific tools and when to use them. It is important to provide students with a variety of tools, materials, and equipment to promote active exploration and inquiry as they begin learning the steps of the scientific process. Doing so develops students' awareness that scientists use specific equipment to conduct investigations, gather information, and produce valid results. By giving each group a bin with various tools for conducting the experiment, this teacher encourages students to select which item will be most useful in gathering information, promoting their understanding of the purpose and uses of scientific equipment.

26. A: The activity described will help children learn about the role of line in visual art, and also about how to draw different kinds of lines. They will also learn how to use different art tools for drawing lines. The children will learn more from this activity using their own body outlines than one using other shapes (B), because young children prefer activities where they are the focus over activities that do not relate to themselves. The children will also learn about shape, but not more than they will learn about line (C), which is the primary focus of this activity. The children may also learn kinesthetic concepts from posing their bodies in different creative positions, but they will definitely learn about art (D) by learning about line and different kinds of lines, about shape and drawing, and about different art tools for making lines.

27. C: Collaborative teaching. Classrooms with a lead teacher often include a specialized teacher to listen to the lesson then work with special needs children. Other methods are: learning centers or stations in which collaborating teachers are responsible for different areas, assigning special needs students into a resource room, team teaching and/or consultation by the special education teacher to the classroom teacher.

28. A: Preschoolers do naturally form stereotypes about others. According to Piaget, children aged 3–6 years are in the Preoperational stage and do not think logically yet. Thus, they tend to base opinions about others on aspects they can see, like people's appearances, the material things they own, or what things they like or dislike. This is natural during their stage of cognitive development; thus (B) is inaccurate. Stereotyping is considered a natural process for children this age rather than something they are taught to do (C). It is also inaccurate to say preschoolers do not understand stereotyping as an abstract concept (D): Preoperational children are cognitively able to categorize people as well as things, and stereotyping or typecasting other people is a form of categorization. Parents and EC educators can reduce stereotyping through modeling, discussion, answering children's questions honestly, promoting tolerance and respect, and confronting biased and intolerant actions.

29. A: As students engage in the artistic process of Creating, the teacher's introduction of other students' artworks facilitates their generalizing or transferring what they have learned about this process to the artistic process of Responding when they experience others' creations. (B) has this backward. The Analysis process involves understanding the individual components of an artwork, and seeing how they come together to appreciate the work as a whole (C); the Interpretation {(C), (D)} process involves constructing meaning from experiencing the art. The Evaluation process (D) involves assessing the quality of an artwork.

30. B: Using additional visual aids and hand gestures will help get your points across more clearly. Answer A is inappropriate. The parents should not have to pay for a translator, and such a strategy would also not encourage the student to increase her English skills. Answer C would make it even harder for the student to understand. Answer D would be unfair to the other students, since it would greatly slow down you class and make it impossible to you to cover your material on schedule.

31. B: Studies do show that although four-year-olds are unlikely to have mastered either print or word concepts, they may have learned many print concepts earlier than word concepts. The most common age for normally developing children to develop print awareness is between three and five years, not five and seven years (A). Studies show that preschoolers who attain print literacy skills ARE more likely to read better when they are older (C). Print awareness is defined as not only knowing that print has meaning, but also understanding the form and function of print (D).

32. A: Toddlers are typically in Erikson's psychosocial stage centering on the nuclear conflict of Autonomy vs. Shame and Self-Doubt. The toddler who shouts "NO!" and has tantrums is exhibiting normal behaviors as s/he works to develop independence (autonomy). Children developing Initiative (B) vs. Guilt are in a later stage, as are children developing Industry (C) vs. Inferiority. Children developing Basic Trust vs. Mistrust (D) are typically the earlier stage of infancy.

33. C: When the teacher lets children choose their favorite colors of stickers, they are getting practice for the future collection of data. When they match their sticker colors to corresponding colors on a piece of poster board, they are getting practice in the future organization of data. And when they see their and the other children's stickers placed on this poster as a chart that everybody can see, they are getting practice for their future display of data they have collected and organized. Identifying sticker shapes (A) is more relevant to learning figure properties. Guessing how many stickers of each color were chosen (B) is more relevant to practice in predicting probabilities. Choosing stickers as rewards for something until they accumulate enough to receive a larger reward (D) is more relevant to a token economy, used in behaviorism to increase the incidence of desired behaviors and decrease undesired ones.

34. A: When preschool teachers assign cooperative activities, children can learn to verbalize what they want. They can learn empathy (B) through discussion and question-answer groups. They can learn cooperation through small-group collaborative projects their teachers assign (C), as well as how to take turns (D), listen to others, and express what they want verbally.

35. A: After approaching calmly, stopping any behaviors that cause physical or emotional harm (step 1), and acknowledging the children's feelings (step 2), the third step in this conflict-mediation/resolution process* is to accumulate as much information as is necessary about the particular conflict from the involved parties. The fourth step is for the mediator to reiterate or restate what the problem is (C). The fifth step is to ask the involved children to think of and suggest potential solutions to the problem identified, and then help them agree to one selected solution (B). The sixth step is to follow up the conflict resolution by providing the involved parties with whatever support they need (D). *[from the HighScope Educational Research Foundation]

36. C: Children develop phonological awareness through a combination of incidental learning via being naturally exposed to language in their environments, and receiving direct instruction from adults. They do not develop it solely through one or the other, or neither.

37. D: Assigning students to write an essay comparing and contrasting the influence that two famous American artists or artworks had on US society would be most appropriate for helping high school students develop an appreciation for the value and role of art in US society. The other activities mentioned, including having students create a slide show presentation about a famous American artist, asking students to create a timeline showing when famous works of American art were created, and taking students on a field trip to an art museum, would not necessarily achieve this learning goal because they do not include it explicitly.

38. A: Integrating technology into instruction must support curriculum goals. Four essential elements of learning that technology must support are connections with real-life experts (a); active student engagement, not passive (b); group participation by students (c); and not only frequent student interaction, but also frequent feedback to students (d).

39. D: Second-grade students can reasonably be expected to have the gross motor skills necessary to participate in a variety of games that require physical activity. Students of this age are developing an increased sense of control over their bodies, and thus benefit from active learning opportunities that allow them to practice coordinated large-muscle movements. In addition, second-grade students have reached the collaborative play stage of development. As such, they can meaningfully participate in, benefit from, and often prefer organized cooperative learning experiences that involve larger groups of students. Interactive group games, such as kickball or follow-the-leader, can best facilitate this preferred learning style while promoting second-grade students' coordination of purposeful body movements.

40. C: The context in which reading occurs poses significant implications on students' overall interest and understanding. As such, it is important that teachers are responsive to students' needs to provide an environment that encourages reading and facilitates comprehension. While in some instances, a quiet area in the classroom dedicated to reading is ideal, young children also benefit from collaborative learning opportunities to build reading comprehension skills. Literature circles are a versatile strategy in which students meet with one another in small groups to discuss a text. During these meetings, students can either focus on an assigned text or talk about a book they are reading independently. In this student-led setting, each person is typically given a role related to a specific aspect of the text, thus promoting personal responsibility and ownership over learning for greater engagement. Implementing literature circles in the classroom allows students to verbalize and work through misunderstandings, questions, and thoughts about a text while building upon one another's knowledge in an interactive setting, thus promoting reading comprehension.

41. B: Environmental print refers to letters, numbers, and words that young children are regularly exposed to in their everyday lives, such as traffic signs, logos, and food labels. As students develop early literacy skills, incorporating environmental print into the classroom is highly beneficial in promoting letter and number recognition. Doing so provides familiar examples for identifying letters and numbers that have been taught, therefore strengthening students' connections by placing learning in a relevant and meaningful context. Allowing young children multiple opportunities to interact with environmental print helps build their understanding that written letters, numbers, and words convey meaning, thus establishing a foundation for developing emergent reading skills.

42. A: Understanding opportunity cost, or the notion that making one choice typically requires sacrificing the potential benefits of another, is important for developing economic literacy. Effectively weighing opportunity costs requires individuals to make well-thought-out choices, so instructional activities related to this concept should incorporate opportunities for students to practice doing so. Implementing a collaborative think-aloud activity would allow students to work through the decision-making process by verbalizing the advantages and disadvantages of their choices with a classmate. Such an activity would serve to enhance students' understanding of the idea that choices have consequences while strengthening their ability to make informed decisions.

43. A: While there is no consensus among experts as to any universal sequence of instruction for teaching the alphabetic principle through phonics instruction, they do agree that, to enable children to start reading words as soon as possible, the highest-utility relationships should be introduced earliest. For example, the letters *m, a, p, t,* and *s* are all used frequently, whereas the *x* in *box*, the sound of *ey* in *they*, and the letter *a* when pronounced as it is in *want* have lower-utility letter-sound correspondences. Important considerations for the alphabetic principle are to teach letter-sound correspondences in isolation, not in word contexts; to teach them explicitly; to give students opportunities to practice letter-sound relationships within their other daily lessons, not only separately; and to include cumulative reviews of relationships taught earlier along with new ones in practice opportunities.

44. A: Teaching young children how to repurpose discarded items shows the concept of recycling as a form of waste management. Doing so demonstrates in a developmentally appropriate context how waste is generated, and how individuals can reduce it to protect the environment. Integrating this concept into daily activities, such as art projects, develops students' understanding of how recycling contributes to managing waste, while encouraging their sense of personal responsibility toward caring for the environment.

45. B: During Piaget's second, Preoperational stage, toddlers and preschoolers' thinking is primarily intuitive, as opposed to being logical (A); logic does not develop until later. Primarily sensory (C) and motoric (D) bases of thought are more closely associated with Piaget's first, Sensorimotor stage of cognitive development during infancy.